JACK EATON
Great Scott! I rhyme a lot.

Jack Eaton: Great Scott! I rhyme a lot.
Published by Memphis Sport Magazine, LLC
Publisher: Mike Bullard
Graphic Design: Mike Bullard, www.abullinachinashop.com
Editing: Mike Bullard, Laura Blanton, Kim Bullard and Kevin Cerrito
Memphis, Tennessee www.memphissport.net

 Copyright © 2008 by Memphis Sport

For information write:
Memphis Sport
1138 N Germantown Pkwy, Ste 101-176, Cordova, TN 38016

ISBN: 978-0-615-24605-5

dedication

Dedicated to the late Mori Greiner,

my boss at Channel 5. Mori was the station general manager. He graduated from Duke but spent his first three years at Washington and Jefferson College-my alma mater. He allowed me to read my poems on Action News 5 and actually encouraged me a few times. Without him, I would not be The Bard of Union Avenue.

Contents

Ode to Jack "THE GREAT"

Would I write the forward for his book?
I said that I would give it a look.
Sorry Jack, I tried to do better
But me thinks I'd better stick to weather.

Dave Brown, Mason Granger, Kim Hindrew and Jack Eaton

I had the pleasure of working on the same news team for almost twenty years with my good friend Jack Eaton. Jack has always been fun to be around. He has one of those great senses of humor. I once heard him say, "I hope I never grow up." I don't think either of us ever did.

He starred in basketball as a 6'7" center at Washington & Jefferson College in Washington, Pennsylvania. But he always said that W&J did not exactly "retire" his jersey, more like they buried it out behind the gym.

forward

He joined WMC shortly after a stint in the U.S. Air Force. He said he spent the Korean War in Puerto Rico and performed his job so magnificently that Puerto Rico was never invaded by the North Koreans.

He knows sports. I can even forgive him for being a Pirates fan, since they are not in the same division as my Cardinals. He is THE legendary television sports anchor of Memphis and the Mid-South, a true pioneer who came on board when television was still in its formative years.

Most folks also remember Jack as the long-time "Voice of the Memphis Tigers" on WMC Radio. He was sometimes criticized for being an unabashed Tiger fan on the air. But, if I may borrow Jack's favorite phrase, GREAT SCOTT…he was talking to Tiger fans, not Louisville or Marquette or UCLA fans. Many of us would watch the game on television while listening to Jack on the radio. I can confirm that he was an outstanding play-by-play man. He knew the game, the players and the fans. He entertained every time he turned on the microphone.

When Jack would fire a zinger at a co-worker, he was delighted when they would pick up on it and fire right back. He soon established the "two second limit" during which you had to respond or you got no credit for the rejoinder. Though they are numerous, one of my favorites was when our chief editor said something to question Jack's knowledge of a subject. Jack said, "Great Scott, Boris, do you think I am a blithering idiot?" Without missing a beat, Boris replied, "Spell blithering."

Jack's poems became a regular staple on Action News 5 on WMC-TV. It all began one night when news anchor Dick Hawley told Jack, "You should write a poem about it." I don't remember the subject, but the poetry soon flowed about many subjects.

We would all be ready for a laugh when Jack would announce to anchor Mason Granger and the entire Mid-South, "Great Scott Mason (he said that a lot), I was so inspired by (whatever the subject) that I wrote a poem about it." Then Jack would read the poem as the text was typed onto the television screen. Most would end with a funny final line.

Jack's poems became legendary.

He regularly waxes poetic in Memphis Sport Magazine and on memphisport.net. He even wrote and delivered a rare poem commercial for Ashley Furniture during our beloved Memphis Tigers' run for the national championship in 2008.

At WMC, we can sometimes prevail on him to return to our studios for a poem in honor of a special event. We have dubbed him, "The Bard of Union Avenue." I hope you can tell that we love the guy!

So get ready to be entertained. He is more conservative than Carl Sandberg, more conventional than E. E. Cummings, easier to decipher than Bob Dylan and much funnier than that Shakespeare guy. Ladies, gentlemen and children of all ages... the poetry of my friend...JACK EATON!

Dave Brown
Weather Director, WMC-TV, Memphis, TN

JACK EATON
Great Scott! I rhyme a lot.

Jack Eaton on Baseball

Great Scott, Michael Jordan's In Town

May 31, 1994

I hope you'll believe me when I say
I thought I wanted to see Michael play.

I love the guy; I'm his biggest fan.
What else can I say, he's my man.

But on my way to the park I thought, "I'm a son of a gun.
Watching him play baseball won't be any fun."

On the basketball court he stands tall and proud,
Clearly above the rest of the crowd.

But on the baseball diamond, at least in my eyes,
He's just another one of the guys.

I'm sorry he left the Bulls, but I'm not bitter,
Although I wish he were more than a .202 hitter.

Michael, I know you march to a different drummer,
And I hope you have a pleasant summer,

But get the heck out of Dodge when the season ends.
Hustle back to Chicago and make amends.

Because you and the Bulls must mightily strive,
Not for four in a row, but for four out of five.

Fanfare
May 31, 1994

I don't care what they say
This is the quote for the month of May.

The Dodger's manager went for a jog
When a fan yelled, "Hey Tommy, Strawberry's a dog."

Lasorda said, "That's not true at all,
A dog is loyal and will chase a ball."

I'm Not the Fan I Used to Be
April 11, 1995

When the baseball strike started I couldn't decide whether
I hoped they'd settle it or quit altogether.

I had been losing interest fast and it wasn't the same;
The players spent more time griping than playing the game.

And the owners acted like a bunch of jerks,
Always trying to foul up the works.

And when they cancelled the series I thought, what's the use?
Let 'em both stew in each others' juice.

The grand old game has been debased and defamed,
And I'll bet Joe and Ted are really ashamed.

So the strike is over and the sides have parted,
To heck with them—my strike has just started.

Things I'm Tired of
July 19, 1995

A baseball strike will be unique;
The players have the owners up the creek.

The players' demands are cut and dried,
And they say they must be satisfied.

If not they'll strike, raise the fist,
And here's where it all takes a different twist.

The millionaire players will just buy a sign
And hire someone to walk the picket line.

This way when it ends, we'll all surely know
The players will be rested and ready to go.

The Boston Red Sox and the Almighty
August 30, 1998

Over the years we've asked for many things:
Batting titles, Cy Youngs, and championship rings.

You've been generous with hitters, Heaven knows,
And our Cy Young awards are lined up in rows.

But no matter how hard we work and strive,
We're still waiting for those wonderful rings to arrive.

This could be our year, but we can't do it alone;
The Yankees are too good, and we are accident prone.

So when the playoffs start, all we ask
Is please make sure we are up to the task.

And if there were a few speed bumps on the New York road,
That would go a long way towards easing our load.

And from the Book of Proverbs, the words we cherish
"A false witness will not go unpunished, and he who speaks
lies will perish."

It Won't Get Any Better Than This
September 9, 1998

As I sat last night in my East Memphis den,
I knew the question wasn't if–but when.

Mark McGuire would open that magic door
And go where no baseball player had gone before.

Then–BINGO–there it was, the record was broken
And though no words need be spoken,

The world went wild, as though quenching a thirst
Because it was so good to see a nice guy finish first.

World Series Wrap-Up
October 28, 1999

If there is one thing an Atlanta fan truly craves
It's another World Series win by the hometown Braves.

They lost this year and I'm calling a halt
To all those who say it was the manager's fault.

I've analyzed the games from bottom to top
And here and now it's time to stop.

His strategy was flawless and his leadership true
It was the players who didn't do what they had to do.

Yes, the Braves were weak when they came to bat
But give the Yankees some of the credit for that.

So, to Bobby Cox's critics I give a loud Bronx cheer
And name him the Jack Eaton Manager of the Year.

Ode to A-Rod
December 13, 2000

Texas shortstop Alex Rodriguez is, as of today,
One of the richest one percent in the USA.

That 252 million really gives me the willies,
Because he's now worth more than the Philadelphia Phillies,

And if invested at ten percent, I think it's true,
He could buy most of what is now Peru.

But AL pitchers say, "What the heck,
He can't hit a baseball with a cashier's check.

And if he comes around with that millionaire's strut
We'll pitch high and inside and knock him on his butt."

So now it's up to A-Rod to move Heaven and Earth
And make sure the Rangers get their money's worth.

But worth it or not, whether he's a bum or a star,
A-Rod has forever raised the salary bar.

A Red Sox Fan's Meditation

February 19, 2004

Oh Lord we can't say for sure that this is true
But we think the Yankees made a pact with you know who.

With A-Rod in their line-up, you've gotta know
That they're the equal of the '27 Murders Row.

If they get a little pitching, who is to say
They won't wrap up the pennant by Labor Day?

So to counter this, it is our contention
That we will need some divine intervention.

Now, we mean A-Rod no real harm,
But if temporarily you were to give him a scatter arm…

And it would be nice, really great,
If he had double vision when he came to home plate.

And for dead solid sure we would love
To see a big hole in that Gold Glove.

So that's about it, nothing more to discuss,
If you'll do that, you can leave the rest to us.

Life's Ups and Downs
May 3, 2008

Some people go through life with relative ease.
It's a piece of cake, a gentle breeze.

They'll pick a stock and buy and buy,
The darn thing goes to a ten year high.

It's at the casino where they really rake in the dough
Every slot machine comes up three cherry's in a row.

At the blackjack table it is almost a must
When things get tough, the dealer goes bust.

And at the racetrack they always seems to know
Where they should bet—win, place or show.

I can only imagine such wheeling and dealing
Because I have a somewhat different feeling.

You see, I have been cursed as an also ran.
I am—Heaven help me—a Pittsburgh Pirates fan.

A Yankee Haters Celebration
May 19, 2008

In the AL East they're havin' a ball
Cause the Yankees can look up and see 'em all.

New York fans are frantic, fit to be hung
If it were a ladder they'd be the bottom rung.

They have the ain'ts and they've really been bitten
You see the pitchers ain't pitchin' and the hitters ain't hittin'.

A sympathy card would be nice if one was so inclined
But few around here are of that frame of mind.

The Red Sox are doing better, they're a little bit higher
But they're not exactly setting the woods on fire.

Boston fans are hopeful and if simply put
We hope the Yanks keep shooting themselves in the foot.

Jack Eaton on the NFL

Be Still, My Beating Heart
May 3, 1994

I'm charged up again because I see from news flashes
That the Hound Dogs, like the Phoenix, may rise from the
ashes.

When the NFL hit us upside the head,
I figured our pro football prospects were dead.

But CBS stepped in and said, "Hold the phone.
You folks are not in this alone."

They lined up Fred Smith and other heavy hitters,
A select group of guys who certainly aren't quitters.

We'll form our own league and then we'll tout it.
And there is nothing the NFL can do about it.

Hey Tagliabue, you jerk, take your league and stick it.
I'm going to call the Hound Dogs and buy a ticket.

I'm Still Mad a Year Later
October 11, 1994

I'll bet that somewhere in the NFL they laughed and laughed
When Jacksonville got the team and we got the shaft.

Now I'll admit that I'm not the fan I used to be
Because, among other things, it occurred to me:

You can tell when an NFL team is on a roll
When they're close enough to kick a boring field goal.

And if you observe very carefully you just might catch
How much the NFL resembles a wrestling match.

And if you run all the numbers you can possibly get,
Notice how many times the underdog is the better bet.

So that's it, NFL, take your money and clout.
Me? I'm an Arena League fan from here on out.

The NFL Draft—Is the End Near?
April 25, 1995

There is a suspicion that the world will not be the same,
Since Alcorn State had a player picked before Notre Dame.

A New Name for the Oilers
July 24, 1997

If I were to give it half a mind,
I'll bet that somewhere I could find

A name that would be a real go-getter
And would say, Tennessee, a whole lot better.

The name they brought to us from Texas
Will be here, I'm sure, forever to vex us.

Oilers–hey, that's not us–unless you mean
The cottonseed kind or maybe soybean.

But in searching for a new name, I became confused
Because all the canines and felines were already used.

So, a connection with the river seemed the way to go
But here and now I want you to know

I decided that's not what we're about.
So, I crossed off catfish, bass and rainbow trout.

Now where do I stand? Which name is best?
As, I am about to conclude my quest.

We need a name that defines us, says who we are,
And will be instantly recognized both near and far.

There is such a name. Yes, Sir and yes, Maam.
Let's call our team the Tennessee Traffic Jam.

Ode to the Oilers
September 25, 1997

Many people have had it with 'em, if you haven't heard,
And their feelings can be summed up in one little word.

So pay close attention and listen up, dude.
That word starts with an *S* and rhymes with "rude."

Their operation never did get off the ground
As local fans got the royal runaround.

The Oilers were arrogant, obnoxious, and unforgiving,
And they thought Memphis owed them a living.

Hey, they're Nashville's team, and if they're so great
Why are there no traffic jams on the interstate?

And the way they left Texas is in some doubt.
Did they leave on their own or did Houston throw them out?

So we don't owe them anything, that's my report,
And they're darn well gonna have to earn our support.

And the message, I think, is loud and clear:
Hey Tagliabue, you geek, stick your league in your ear.

The Forward Pass
That Was Called a Lateral
January 10, 2000

In the annals of football it will stand alone
And will someday be carved in solid stone.

The Bills were cheated, it's as simple as that,
Because if that was a lateral, I'll eat my hat.

Here's what happened, pay close attention,
Because I was an eyewitness and it's my contention,

Though the play was well planned with clever disguise
And caught the Buffalo Bills by surprise,

That wasn't a lateral, as the videotape proved,
But the official on the field clearly was not moved.

He ruled a touchdown and the Titans advanced
But against the Colts, they don't have a chance.

The Bills were robbed, I emphatically restate,
And I call for Jesse Jackson to investigate.

The Big Game
January 11, 2000

The purpose of the following is to inform and enlighten
For the upcoming game between the Colts and the Titans.

I doubt there is any amount of careful planning
That will allow the Titans to stop Peyton Manning.

Now, the Colts have had two weeks to rest and prepare,
And this spells trouble for Steve McNair.

To my way of thinking, it's a pretty safe bet
The Colts will take away the Titans' deep threat.

So with the passing game kaput, it's an easy call:
Eddie George will have to run the ball.

And in my analysis I'm here to report,
The Colts defense will be able to hold the fort.

So in conclusion, here is my pre-game slant:
Eddie George won't win it, Air McNair can't.

Super Bowl—An Ode To

January 31, 2000

The Tennessee Titans, as of today,
Should be the champions of all they survey.

The St. Louis Rams were ripe for the picking
And should have been given a big-time licking.

But the Titans made one mistake that sealed their fate–
They began to run the ball too late.

The Rams led 16-0 and the Tennessee outlook was grim
When the coach pointed to Eddie and said, "Give the ball to him."

And before St. Louis could run and hide,
All of a sudden the game was tied.

But give the Rams credit, they turned on the juice
And got the football to Isaac Bruce.

So hats off to the Rams, but you and I know
That running the football is the way to go.

The Manning Factor
April 26, 2004

The NFL draft is very special, always a big deal,
But this year it was even better, I gotta feel.

The process was given an extra boost
When the Archie Manning factor was introduced.

The San Diego Chargers had the number one pick,
And that they might take Eli made Archie sick.

Because after studying the team, he was ready to state
The whole organization was second rate.

So after the Chargers drafted Eli, they looked for a trade,
And a deal with the Giants was quickly made.

So my hat's off to Archie, he did what he could,
And as Sonny Boy would say, "Archie, you done good."

Jack Eaton on the SEC

Ode to the Big Game

October 13, 1999

Ole Miss fans will gather from far and wide
To watch their team do battle with the Crimson Tide.

They know the Rebels will have to play like the devil
To take their game to the championship level.

And every Ole Miss fan knows deep in his heart
That beating Alabama is the place to start.

The special teams are important but a vital need
Is for Romero Miller to make the proper read.

Then the defense must dig in and stop the run
While putting Andrew Zow under the gun.

If they all work together and share the load,
The Rebels can get into that winning mode.

And something Ole Miss fans always knew:
When it comes to Alabama, the Rebels are overdue.

NCAA Rules and Regulations, Logan Young, and Enforcement

April 27, 2001

The NCAA will bring Logan Young to his knees
When they prove he sold secrets to the Red Chinese.

In the meantime, they're searching far and wide
To prove he paid players for the Crimson Tide.

Now, the NCAA is known to feel
That selling secrets to the Commies is no big deal.

But paying football players goes beyond the pale
And any perpetrator should surely be put in jail.

But if there is a charge, Logan knows he can lick it,
And tell the NCAA just where they can stick it.

So I think for sure he can stand the heat,
And it looks to me like he's in the driver's seat.

So to the NCAA he can say, "Here's what I'll do:
It starts with an *S* and rhymes with *roo you*."

Miami Dan is Always Right
July 3, 2001

SEC fans are overly chauvinistic, at least
When comparing their football teams to those of the Big East.

They're boastful, crass, and devoid of tact,
And they overlook one all-important fact.

In last season's bowl games, and I know this is true,
Against the Big East the SEC was 0 for 2.

To make sure you know where I'm coming from,
The Mountaineers of WVU beat Ole Miss like a drum.

Then the mighty Florida Gators—my, oh, my—
Were forced by the 'Canes to eat humble pie.

So no more SEC teams, but thanks just the same;
Next year we'll play someone who'll at least make it a game.

A Conference is a Conference is a Conference

July 17, 2001

SEC fans make no secret of the fact,
If it ever became necessary, they would make a pact

With the Devil himself, if that's what it took,
To make sure they looked good in the record book.

But their claim of superiority may be a dream
Or sophistry carried to the ultimate extreme.

The Big East is as good, and across the river,
The Pac 10 and the Big 12 ain't exactly chopped liver.

And coming up is the annual triple whammy:
Oklahoma, Nebraska, and, of course, Miami.

SEC fan loyalty is great but that's the catch:
They always count their chickens before they hatch.

Where Have You Gone, Wayne Madkin?

July 23, 2000

SEC football hasn't been the same
Since Wayne Madkin played his last conference game.

With his exceptional skill he could take the heat,
And he deserves his spot among the nation's elite.

It will be remembered that it was at his behest
That the Bulldogs rose to the top of the SEC West.

In the title game they had the lead, and I said, "Home free,"
But then they were victimized by a terrible referee.

So a conference championship for Wayne was not in the charts,
But he will always remain number one in our hearts.

Albert Means, the SEC, and Illegal Payments
January 15, 2001

First of all, I want to make it perfectly clear,
I've had it with the Albert Means business up to here.

Someone at Alabama is really out of touch
Because two hundred grand for a tackle is way too much.

On top of that, it was terribly unfair;
Hey, Albert never even got a share.

And when the story broke, the kid didn't run and hide;
He went straight to Tuscaloosa and quit the Crimson Tide.

So what's Albert's next move? Where will he play?
No one knows, but I think it's safe to say,

Wherever he goes this one last time,
It won't cost anybody one thin dime.

Meanwhile those Alabama guys are really stunned,
They're wondering if they might get a full refund.

I Like the BCS

December 8, 2003

The BCS is the best we can do;
Unless there is a playoff, this is true.

And since there won't be a playoff anytime soon,
Let's all get together and hum the same tune.

There are lots of folks who honestly feel
That Southern Cal got a really lousy deal.

The two wire service polls had the Trojans number one,
But the computer computed and when it was all said and done

LSU and Oklahoma were named to play in the Sugar Bowl,
And the winner will be the team with the highest payroll.

In that case, I can definitely say to you,
No one has a payroll higher than LSU.

Jack Eaton on UT

A Volunteer Fans Prayer
June 2, 1998

We approach the Almighty with bended knee
And we ask that he not bring us home scot-free.

No, just help us to meet every test
And make sure we do our dead level best.

Help Tee Martin read defenses with eagle eyes
and pick apart what the enemy's trying to disguise.

We know that Jamal Lewis is a great running back
But, give him an extra push at the point of attack.

Then help Phil Fulmer keep his mind on the game
By giving him the wisdom of King "What's-His-Name."

If you do that we'll all say grace
And keep guys like Weinberger firmly in place.

A Pre-Game Letter to Coach Fulmer

September 15, 1999

Coach, you haven't asked, but I thought it nice
If I were to offer some sage advice.

I have three things to say, so here's my call:
Run the ball, run the ball and run the ball.

Keep the pressure on. Never stop,
Even when Jamal is too pooped to pop.

When you throw the ball, you can be had.
Three things can happen and two are bad.

So keep the ball on the ground. No ifs, ands or buts.
And play General Patton's defense—you know—blood and guts.

If you'll do that you'll look a whole lot wiser
And laugh as Coach Spurrier eats his visor.

I Told You So
November 9, 1999

50%

As I contemplated the Vols clash with Notre Dame,
I remember saying it would'nt be a very close game.

Tennessee was too quick and had a lot more power
And they'd knock the Irish off their ivory tower.

35 to 7 was the final score I chose
And surely by now, everyone knows

That 38 to 14 was the actual score.
So, the margin was not 28, just 24.

I was feeling so smart when I remembered this,
I also picked the Tigers to beat Southern Miss.

But, alas, I know this is true.
Fifty percent is better than I usually do.

The First Football Poem of the Season
May 15, 2000

I know it's only the middle of May,
And football season is still a few months away,

But I've been thinking about the Tennessee Volunteers
And how to boost their standing among their peers.

They'll be inexperienced at quarterback, so it would be great
If they could make a trade for Wayne Madkin of Mississippi State.

Put all of that Tennessee talent at his beck and call,
And all the coach would have to do is say, "Play ball."

There is no doubt in my mind that's all it would take,
And winning the national title would be a piece of cake.

Then his most ardent fans could make the case
To change Peyton Manning Pass to Wayne Madkin Place.

Florida 27, Tennessee 23

September 18, 2000

Looking back at the first half, all I can say,
The Volunteers should have blown the Gators away.

Four trips to the red zone and like it or not,
Four lousy field goals was all that they got

To a football purist, that's a cardinal sin.
And as such, the Vols didn't deserve to win.

Give Florida credit, because it occurred to me
Their defense was tough when it had to be.

Suggs did well and Travis Henry played tough,
But their efforts, however, just weren't good enough.

So it seems that Coach Fulmer's pre-ordained fate
Is to be forever known as Gator bait.

Tennessee vs. Florida—An Analysis

September 19, 2003

A year ago the Gators had a win to savor,
But this year the Vols should return the favor.

My advice to Tennessee is basically sound:
To win, you've gotta keep the ball on the ground.

Give Cedric Houston 30 touches, maybe 35,
And then Casey Clausen will eat the Gators alive.

So first run, then pass, establish a groove
And I'd bet that even General Neyland would approve.

So Coach Fulmer, if you'll do just as I say,
I can almost guarantee that you'll come away

With a win that'll be one for the book,
And also, your first-ever over Coach Ron Zook.

Tennessee 10, Miami 6

November 10, 2003

For Hurricanes fans it was tough to endure,
But the one thing the game did for sure

Was to put Phil Fulmer's status above reproach
And guarantee his spot as a great football coach.

He had his Volunteers primed and ready;
The coach's eyes were clear, his hand was steady.

He knew that to win, he had to be an honest broker
And do a better coaching job than Larry Coker.

He urged the defense to crank it up one level
And just like that—sure as the devil—

They forced enough turnovers that at the end of the day,
"The 'Canes did theirselves in," as Coach Murphy would say.

So hail to Phil Fulmer, and whether he knows it or not,
He proved that Jeff Weinberger don't know squat.

Tennessee Paranoia

July 29, 2004

Media Day in Birmingham is a really big deal,
But to Phil Fulmer, it has absolutely no appeal.

The UT coach was not at all vague;
He avoided the thing like the bubonic plague

He said he stayed home because he lost his fervor,
But he really wanted to dodge the process server.

Bama fans dislike Fulmer because they think
He's a bad guy, a truly despicable fink.

They say Fulmer called the NCAA a while ago
And told them things about the Tide they wanted to know.

And he had a good reason, or so it seems to me,
By squealing on Alabama, he took the heat off Tennessee.

But now Crimson Tide fans are saying, "Thank the Lord,"
Because all this will look great on the Bama bulletin board.

College Football—Nothing Like It
November 15, 2005

Great Caesar's Ghost and golly gee whiz,
Fulmer doesn't know who his best quarterback is.

But cut him some slack, because it's understood
That neither Clausen nor Ainge is very good.

So without an engineer to drive the train,
The UT season is pretty much down the drain.

It's not a matter of money, the Vols have more
Than the gross domestic product of El Salvador.

And Fulmer's program is as clean as the white Florida sand
They dropped out of the Means' bidding at 75 grand.

So no one in Knoxville is sure what should be done;
No matter, they're all back at square number one.

Meanwhile, the Hurricane season is a bright pure gem;
It won't be any Shreveport Independence Bowl for them.

So all of us Miami fans, raise our glasses high
To all of the UT fans—here's mud in your eye.

Jack Eaton on Tiger Football

Some people think Jack Eaton leans a little towards Memphis State in his sportscasts.

Maybe he does. But Jack's evident enthusiasm for the Memphis State Tigers falls on receptive ears.

He modestly admits that he's not the nation's best play-by-play man, "only somewhere in the top one or two." (In a recent survey, Memphians overwhelmingly named him their favorite local sportscaster.)

Memphians like WMC-TV News because they get more newsfilm, more documentaries, more community involvement. They also get more Memphis State sports news, and— Great Scot!—what more could you want?

wmctv5

51

Nothin' Is Easy
September 27, 2004

It can now be unequivocally stated
That Joe Lee Dunn's defense is overrated.

Please put this stat in your memory file:
The last two opponents have gained three-fourths of a mile.

The Arkansas State game was bad, but UAB?
They lit up the Tigers like a Christmas tree.

And this number should get your nose out of joint:
The Indians and Blazers combined for 70 points.

So as I view the carnage, here's my call,
I'm reminded of Rome—you know the rise and fall.

But hang in there, Tiger fans, and please take heart,
Because basketball season is soon to start.

Esoteric Baloney
October 18, 1994

When one of my predictions doesn't come to pass,
  I would like it described with a little class.

Instead of saying–WRONG–which sounds like a blight,
  How much better to say, "It was other than right."

It's a kinder and gentler environment that I seek,
  Because I'll be back predicting in another week.

I'm going to pick the Tigers, and if they get burnt,
  Don't say, "They got beat." Try, "Winner they weren't."

And about Tiger football, there is one sure bet–
  Parking spaces are certainly easy to get.

It's Ole Miss Week
November 1, 1994

Tiger fans will reluctantly confess
That playing in Oxford, their team's had little success.

Actually their luck has been the worst,
And their next win at Vaught-Hemingway will be their first.

So as we approach this year's crucial hour,
We need help and guidance from a higher power.

Oh, heaven above, we pray the most
Their every field goal hits the post.

And when the Rebs get the ball, could you make it rain?
And add about a yard to the first-down chain?

That's about it except for this:
If you can't help us, don't help Ole Miss.

I'm aware of the odds and what everyone thinks,
But I predict the Tigers will break that Oxford jinx.

Ode To The Tigers
November 15, 1994

All year-long it has been the Tigers' goal
To end the season with a bid to the Liberty Bowl.

Right now they're so close they can almost taste it;
It's a golden opportunity and they dare not waste it.

It all comes down to Saturday's final game;
If they don't make it, they've only themselves to blame.

They'll play East Carolina, and I ask, who?
It sounds like a new name for the Asian flu.

But they like their chances, to which I say,
Cool it, Pirates, there ain't no way.

The Tigers will win, I'm confident of that,
And if they don't, I swear I'll eat my hat.

The Tigers' Last Hurrah
November 22, 1994

I thought it would be exciting, interesting, and fun,
But it turned out a bummer–the wrong team won.

I was surprised that the Tigers, with only four defeats,
Would have so many fans disguised as empty seats.

I figured the U of M would win if they turned up the heat,
And I promised to eat my hat if they got beat.

That the Tigers lose the "big one" is not really new,
But I figured at last they just might be due.

But one thing happened that a Tiger fan dreads–
The defense was manhandled and ripped to shreds.

So it was a great disappointment, what more can be said?
But I'll not eat my hat, I'll bury it instead.

Save the Tigers

December 13, 1994

orange

Over the weekend I was distressed and saddened to learn
That the future of Tiger football is of great concern.

They can't attract fans as hard as they try,
And in the president's office they're wondering why.

I have pondered their predicament and have a solution
Though it might be the cause of a small revolution.

The problem is color, and it might seem strange,
But I think the Tigers would do well to change.

Suppose they wore orange, what a difference it could make
As thousands of UT fans showed up by mistake.

The whole thing wouldn't be a whole lot of fun
But at least Tiger fans would see how it's done.

The New Orleans Bowl—Go, Tigers, Go

December 15, 2003

It's not the Orange Bowl, the Cotton, or even the Rose,
But deep down inside every Tiger fan knows

That it's time for the U of M to shift its gears
And head for post-season play for the first time in years.

It may not be the BCS, but all Tiger fans say,
We love New Orleans so it's A-OK.

The Tigers play North Texas and this you should know:
The Mean Green won their last eight games in a row.

They lost to Oklahoma, Air Force, and the Razorbacks
Everyone else they stopped dead in their tracks.

Now the Tigers can win and win going away
If Danny Wimprine remembers how well he can play.

Read those defenses, Danny, and follow the gameplan.
And for heaven's sake, only throw to the open man.

So if the Tigers hang onto the ball all the while,
And Joe Lee's boys play defense like it's going out of style,

The Tigers will enjoy a New Orleans feast
And win by a couple of touchdowns, at least.

So go for broke Tigers, roll those dice,
And if you win for Coach Murphy, that would be nice.

Tigers vs. Nicholls State
September 16, 2008

When your team's 0 and 3 you've taken enough jibes
So what you need are lots of positive vibes.

It's now time I think to take a different tack
So here is some free advice from–Great Scott–Big Jack.

In the Red Zone you can keep 'em at bay
By using the old Statue of Liberty play.

If that doesn't work there is one other thing
You might line up in the old UT single wing.

I promise you to Nicholls State it would look brand new
And they would have no idea what they should do.

Now this might sound like I fell out of a tree
But remember right now you are 0 and 3.

So give it a shot. Go with the flow.
As for me it's easy–Go Tigers. Go..

Jack Eaton on the NBA

Ode To the NBA
May 10, 1994

Concerning the Rookie of the Year, here's the word:
It was the worst decision I've ever heard.

Chris Webber is tough when he posts up in the paint,
But, let's face it fans, Anfernee Hardaway he ain't.

Penny can do it all—run, pass, and shoot.
And if that's not enough he'll steal the ball to boot.

His talents are many and do you know what he'll do?
Lead the Magic to the championship before he is through.

So Penny, you're not the Rookie of the Year, but praise the Lord,
You've just won the first annual Jack Eaton Award.

I have been watching the playoffs, and I'm a son of a gun—
So far it hasn't been a barrel of fun.

I picked Seattle in the West, and Great Caesar's Ghost,
Denver knocked them from pillar to post.

It was a terrible prediction, and I know why
On that particular day both pollen and mold were
abnormally high.

Ode To Penny

October 25, 1994

Anfernee Hardaway has walked the path,
And now all Treadwell kids are studying math.

Penny's their hero, he showed the way,
And he made the Magic pay and pay.

When it comes to the deal, Anfernee knows how it's done,
So his contract with Orlando is second to none.

Oh, Shaq makes more after incentives and such;
But I'm told the difference isn't very much.

So with everything in place, the Magic makes it's run,
And I'd guess that Anfernee feels under the gun.

Each game is vital, and they'll sure try to win it,
But either way Anfernee makes $1400 a minute.

The NBA Champions—Remember Where You Heard It

May 23, 1995

The Magic started out with a heavy load;
The experts said they couldn't win on the road,

But they gave a hint of what was in store
By beating the Celtics twice on the parquet floor.

Then the Bulls' series had a familiar ring;
Orlando went to Chicago and did the very same thing.

So now it's two series down with two to go.
I've studied it carefully and this much I know:

While the other teams are good, there is one thing they lack,
They just can't match up with Penny and Shaq.

So the Magic have arrived, they are definitely for real,
And they'll win the NBA, that's a done deal.

The Way Things Are
December 9, 1997

Latrell Sprewell would have a lot to gain
By being compared to Saddam Hussein.

Saddam has killed thousands of people just for fun,
While Sprewell's just choked and then only one.

Latrell's no ange, but unlike Saddam
He's not trying to build a nuclear bomb.

And though he's profane, obnoxious and crass
He doesn't have a stockpile of poison gas.

So get off his back because he's taking note
And if you don't, who knows he may just slit your throat.

And, ya know, some of the teams in the NBA
Would sign Saddam if he could hit the outside *J.*

Ode To Dennis Rodman

February 23, 1999

73

My support for the Lakers is now semi-firm
Since they've gone out and signed The Worm.

Rodman is a creep, a weirdo, but I cannot lie,
For some unknown reason I like the guy.

After watching the Lakers, it's a dead even bet—
They're gonna need all the help they can get.

Dennis will get lots of rebounds right off the bat,
But the Lakers need a whole lot more than that.

Rodman can't shoot, and his ball handling is bad,
So my suspicion is, the Lakers have been had.

So instead of a championship, I see a bubble,
Because they're about to get a ton a trouble.

A Tale of Two Frenchman: Napoleon and Tony Parker

May 10, 2004

If you have read much history, you already knew
That Napoleon met his defeat at Waterloo.

It was the Duke of Wellington who made Napoleon wince,
And the French army hasn't won a darn thing since.

We bailed them out of World Wars I and II,
And looking back I'm not sure it was the right thing to do.

A fan of the French I am certainly not,
So you can imagine what a thrill I got

When the Lakers defense finally rose up
And put Tony Parker and Gary Payton's noses up.

Mano y mano was the order of the day,
And it was a price Tony Parker would not pay.

It was gut check time, and I'm happy to report,
Once again a Frenchman came up short.

So, Phil Jackson is a genius, and it will come to pass,
Someday he will be mentioned in Phil Fulmer's class.

Jack Eaton on the Grizzlies

It's Not Likely to Get Much Better Than This

March 26, 2001

I always thought it a big-time pity
That Memphis was not a major league city.

We once hitched our wagon to the NFL's star
And we came oh so close–but no cigar.

They called us, but there were problems involved.
Fred Smith took over, and the problems were solved.

It all came down to a two-city race,
And, happily, Louisville came in second place.

So the Grizzlies are ours, and it's a good guess
That their new name will be the Memphis Express.

My cup runneth over, my joy is extreme.
Great Caesar's Ghost, we have a major league team!

The NBA, Memphis, and What's Right
May 8, 2001

The NBA is taking a good look at us
To see if we're ready for Major League status.

The only thing standing in our way
Is a brand spankin' new place to play.

The NBA is beating its drum;
Build us an arena, and we will come.

So the question for us is: do we have the will
To force taxpayers to pay the bill?

Time is short, and from what I hear
The decision–yay or nay–is very near.

I say, Let's go for it, we'll be passive no more,
And go where no Memphians have ever gone before.

Yogi Was Wrong—It's Over

May 16, 2001

The NBA had Memphis under the gun,
But now it looks like the deal is done.

All the *I*s aren't dotted and the *T*s aren't crossed,
But to the NBA opponents I'd say, "All is lost."

It's the biggest news in Memphis, or so it seems to me,
Since the basketball Tigers signed Keith Lee.

And I'm sure the new owners will move Heaven and Earth
To see that our team gets a playoff berth.

It won't happen next season, though we'll come on strong,
But I'm confident it won't be too very long.

So rejoice, NBA fans, be proud of what you did.
Now let's go out and fill the Pyramid.

Some Days Are Better Than Others
June 28, 2001

For years a major league team has been our goal,
But no one would touch us with a ten-foot pole.

Then suddenly it was almost too good to be true
When the Vancouver Grizzlies appeared out of the blue.

Their trip to Memphis wasn't easy, but today I feel
It's finally a certified blue ribbon deal.

And to say we hit the ground running, I really fear
Would qualify as the understatement of the year.

First Abdur "What's-His-Name" was traded and it was quick,
But we got Lorenzen Wright and Atlanta's first pick.

Then we drafted Battier and a seven footer from Spain,
And today I haven't heard anyone complain.

Then Mike Bibby was traded to the Sacramento Kings
For Jason Williams and all the excitement he brings.

So I'm really pumped up, and I can't understand why
The NBA won't start the season on the Fourth of July.

Weinberger's Law
July 19, 2003

Some Grizzlies fans say they can prove
That Jerry West is about to make a move.

When asked to be more specific, they hem and haw
And mutter something about Weinberger's Law.

Weinberger's Law, what in the world is that?
It turns milk sour and makes tires go flat.

So let's apply it to the Grizzlies' needs
And see where this convoluted logic leads.

Jeff says the team would get a lift
Simply by getting rid of Stromile Swift.

Then he'd line 'em up all in a row–
J. Will, Shane and Pau, they gotta go.

Then they'd get a player Jeff would really love,
A seven footer who can push and shove.

So, Jeff's ideal team comes as no surprise:
Greg Ostertag and four other guys.

Jerry West, Hubie Brown, Coach Murphy, and Sonny Boy
February 9, 2004

As a genius, Jerry West is above reproach
Because he hired Hubie as the Grizzlies coach.

And yesterday Hubie's boys held sway
As they beat the best team in the NBA.

I have to think that the main reason why
Is they finally found their go-to guy.

Pau Gasol is his name, and I want you to hear:
He stuck the ball in the Timberwolves' ear.

But at crunch time Hubie made the definitive call—
He put Shane Battier in the game and gave him the ball.

And once again, the old Dukie shows he's a real go-getter
Because William Tell himself couldn't have shot it better.

So hail to Jerry and Hubie and get outta the way,
"They done theirselves proud," as Coach Murphy would say.

And Sonny Boy would add (if only he could),
"Yeah, those boys, they done real good."

The Dreaded P Word
March 26, 2004

The NBA's regular season is drawing to a close,
And every Grizzlies fan positively knows

That it is a major league bone of contention
For anyone near Jerry West even to mention

That the playoffs are next and, for Heaven's sake,
It's the first time the Grizzlies will partake.

Now superstitious is one thing the Genius ain't.
Still, there is an outside chance that a mention might taint

Our playoff chances, so Jerry used his clout,
And any use of the *P* word is definitely out.

Hey–I want to use the *P* word in the worst kind of way,
But I won't use it, Jerry, until you say it's OK.

Now It's the C Word

March 29, 2004

Now that our playoff drought has been broken,
It's time for the dreaded *P* word to be openly spoken.

And now is the time figuratively to set sail
In search of the NBA's Holy Grail.

At the risk of incurring Jerry West's wrath,
I am now on what may be a lonely path.

I've analyzed everything, and here's my call:
I say we have a good shot to win it all.

We have talented players and a heck of a coach,
And our management team is above reproach.

If that doesn't equal the *C* word, I'll eat my hat;
I want the NBA Championship, it's as simple as that.

It Can't Get a Whole Lot
Better Than This
March 29, 2004

The Grizzlies have entered the NBA's promised land,
But it wasn't Moses, it was Stromile Swift, who took command.

With his great talent he beat Toronto to the draw;
It was the Memphis version of shock and awe.

But now that we're in, no one knows how to act.
We've never been here before, and that's a fact.

But if Hubie were to ask, I'd simply say,
"Give the ball to Stromile and get out of the way."

If his game is off and he falls on the floor,
Hey, that's what Pau and the rest of the guys are for.

To be honest, I haven't had this much fun
Since Maz hit the World Series winning home run.

Ode to the Logo
December 17, 2004

I'm setting out on my one-man quest
To stop all the dogging of Jerry West.

Think for a moment, take a small pause—
When he was hired, the Grizzlies were a total lost cause.

But when he arrived, he quickly took command
And, like Moses, led the Grizzlies to the promised land.

We got 50 wins last season, a heck of a feat,
And we were among the NBA elite.

I'm a Jerry West fan, and it's a darn sure bet
When it comes to the Grizzlies, we ain't seen nothin' yet.

The NBA Lottery-Phooey

May 22, 2008

I tuned in the draft hoping we'd catch a break,
But what did I see for Heaven's Sake.

We came in fifth but some said we had it made,
Because it was at five that Miami got Dwyane Wade.

Now, that may be true but try as we will,
I'd say our chances of that are somewhere near nil.

Hey, if it weren't for bad, here's my call,
We wouldn't have any luck at all.

So I dread next season, we'll take a lot of flack
Because last year was bad and all those guys are back.

It's really depressing and may I add this
We'll be back in the lottery, no way we can miss.

Grizzlies – Wither Thou Goest

May 13, 2008

Grizzlies fans now know what Shakespeare meant
When he wrote of *Our Winter of Discontent.*

Discontent, indeed. Hey, I think I heard
One fan say, "Disaster would be a better word."

The team has suffered so many defeats
That most fans come disguised as empty seats.

Things are so bad that for all I know
They might bring back Big Country and Sidney Lowe.

If the Grizzlies were a stock I'm here to tell
The word on the street would be sell, sell, sell.

On the other end the brokers would wonder why
There was no one willing to buy, buy, buy.

Now, the draft might save us really quick
If we can just get that number one pick.

I'm willing to give our owner the benefit of the doubt
The draft and a good free agent may bail us out.

The whole process has me scared half to death
And to be perfectly frank-I'm not holding my breath.

Jack Eaton on Politics

Ode to Bill and Hillary
April 12, 1994

Bill was upset, Hillary was shaken,
So they decided to have a picture taken.

The photographer said, "Your attention please
Look at the camera and just say *sleeze*."

Ode to Election Night
November 8, 1994

I've seen a lot of elections come and go,
And this one thing I surely know:

The thing I like the very best
Is that they put those TV ads to rest.

The past few weeks have taken their toll,
And I'd have lost my mind without the remote control.

I could hold it here in the palm of my hand,
And when I'd had all of those guys I could stand.

I'd point it at the screen and give it a pop,
And it felt so good, I just can't stop.

Quickly to black—Great Scott!

John Willingham for Mayor

June 8, 2003

A big part of the electorate, I have no doubt,
Has finally had it—they're Willied out.

Whatever will be shall come to pass,
And the mayor comes across as arrogant and crass.

And after 12 long years, it's not all that strange
That many feel it's time for a change.

And a change for the better, yes sir and yes ma'am
Would be to elect good ole John Willingham.

One immediate change that I can see—
He wouldn't try to rule by royal decree.

Willingham is a man of the people and one of the few
Who'd welcome a comparison to a comfortable old shoe.

So Willingham is ready to shoulder the load
And make Memphis, again, the city of good abode.

The Perfect Storm
July 30, 2003

Memphis took a hit but kept on tickin'
With precious little help from Willie the Chicken.

While our work crews labored around the clock,
Our fearless leader was safe in Little Rock.

When asked about it, Willie said, "This is so.
I don't get paid for what I do, but for what I know.

And I know that with trees down as far as the eyes can see,
Memphis just is not the place that I want to be.

And I don't worry about the election, I have such a hold
The voters of Memphis will do just what they are told."

But the feeling around many a Memphis neighborhood is:
Let's send Willie to Little Rock for good.

So my friends, this is now where we are at—
A vote for John Willingham will do just that.

King Willie
January 7, 2004

King Willie's luster began to fade
Right after his New Year's Day tirade.

Watching on television, I swear that I saw
Not an acceptance speech, but a laying down of the law.

The mayor was pompous, pontifical, and even verbose
And if wasn't arrogant, he was awfully close.

He credited God with his position, and if this is so,
It's not the same God that I worship and know.

But then His Honor really missed the boat
When he tried to jam his appointments down the council's throat.

After due deliberation and considerable fuss
They said, "Four of these guys are not OK with us."

So the battle lines have been drawn, and this I know,
Somewhere John Willingham is saying, "I told you so."

Let's Do It To It
January 2005

John Ford or King Willie—which one will be
Named the #@$% stud in Tennessee.

For a long time Senator Ford was in the lead,
But lately our Mayor has drawn a bead.

Mayor Herenton announced his number one bid
When he admitted that he had an illegitimate kid.

Now, when the Senator's heard of Willie's indiscretion,
He said it was time for a true confession.

Ford said his past has really been haunted
Because being mayor is what he's always wanted.

He even said his campaign slogan would certainly be,
I'll get a vasectomy if you'll just elect me.

Ode To Philandering
January 2005

A philanderer is one who likes to roam
And get his nighttime kicks away from home.

Of course, there are philanderers almost everywhere,
But here in Memphis, we seem to have more than our share.

And for some strange reason and I'm not sure why
It is oftentimes a most high profile guy.

Our mayor, it would seem, is too old for that
But now in his 60's, King Willie is a regular tomcat.

He even had an out-of-wedlock kid, but it was no big deal
Because Senator John Ford is known to feel

That it takes persistence and a lot of heart,
And one little bastard is just a good start.

So if we could get these two to a sperm bank—oh how clever—
Because then we'd have both John and Willie around forever.

The Election Of Ophelia Ford
January 2006

The big question around town is, did dead people vote?
Well, Harold Ford Sr. investigated and here is his quote:

"Whether all you white devils like it or not,
This whole thing was a dirty Republican plot."

Now I imagine there are some who are truly relieved
Because they feel that Harold Sr. is to be believed.

Of all the people under God's blue sky,
Why would Ford Sr. deliberately lie?

But there are others who think he is not above libel,
And wouldn't trust him if he were holding a bible.

Those are the two differing views, and if it were to matter,
I strongly come down on the side of the latter.

On Holidays
March 2007

Of all the holiday celebrations, I'd have to say
The most confusing is John Ford's party on Father's Day.

Each year, he tries hard to get it right,
But he never knows how many kids to invite.

The guy is a stud of great renown,
And he spreads his seed all over town.

One thing for sure—and this is a lock—
He's seen more morning sickness than Dr. Spock.

He's good at conception, that's his thrill,
But he's not so hot at paying the bill.

He's in trouble now, and it all took shape
When the FBI caught him stealing on videotape.

If he goes to jail he will surely come to grief,
But the ladies around town will breathe a sigh of relief.

Jack Eaton on Radio

30 Second Promo
May 14, 1999

Hi, this is Jack Eaton, with an invitation for you
To join Jeff Weinberger and me on WHBQ.

If you have a question, we'll gladly take it,
And if we can't answer, we'll probably fake it.

Now, Jeff is an expert, at the front of the line,
But that's his opinion and not necessarily mine.

Be that as it may, our priority number one
Is that our listeners have lots of fun.

So we took a poll, and would you believe
Miami Dan loves us and so does Lexington Steve.

So tune in weekdays from one to three for Jeff and Jack,
And if you're not satisfied, we'll give you your money back.

Ode to Our Number One Caller
July 12, 2000

While some of our callers are throwing up bricks,
Miami Dan is getting in solid licks.

He bides his time; he'll pick and choose
And only call when he cannot lose.

He has facts and figures on his side,
Something that Weinberger just can't abide.

Take the Indianapolis Colts, they had a banner season,
But Dan said Peyton Manning was not the primary reason.

Credit Edgerrin James with what anyone can see—
The Colts went from 3 and 13 to 13 and 3.

I hope he calls up today, and then just maybe
He'll show us again how to take candy from a baby.

The End Is Near

June 25, 2001

It was a perfect afternoon for a leisurely drive,
And we were headed South toward Memphis on I-55.

We were well-within range of Sports56,
So I thought I'd tune in, just for kicks.

And there was Jeff with his latest word,
And it was the most gosh awful thing I'd ever heard.

I'd always considered Dean Smith as being above reproach,
But here was Weinberger saying he was a lousy coach.

Lousy coach, gimme a cotton-pickin' break.
He's the all-time winningest, for Heaven's sake.

I thought to myself, this is the final straw,
And it's time to use the power of Tennessee law.

What I'm accusing you of may seem frivolous to some,
But I'm charging you with being terminally dumb.

You can remain silent if you think that's best,
Because I'm placing you under a citizen's arrest.

There'll be no trial, no appeal—you'll go straight to jail
And spend 30 days cooped up with Duncan Ragsdale.

Stop Before You Start

June 13, 2003

Somehow it always seems to be my fate
To have to listen to Weinberger pontificate.

And his latest crusade, by the way,
Is to downgrade the players in the NBA.

Now the shooting has been off this playoff season,
But there is one persistent, overriding reason.

So, Jeff put this in your stupid file:
These guys play defense like it's going out of style.

And this, above all, is absolutely vital–
Offense sells tickets, but defense wins a title.

So don't even start, you'd better shut your yap.
Like Lexington Steve, I don't want to hear that crap.

Idiots, Idiots, Everywhere
September 15, 2003

How does one know an idiot these days?
As Shakespeare once wrote, "Let me count the ways."

An idiot will often, as strange as it seems,
Find fault with offensive blocking schemes.

Then they will, whether we like it or not,
Claim that Pau Gasol can't create his own shot.

Another favorite ploy, I want you to hear,
Is to criticize Wayne Madkin's brilliant career.

The one thing above all I really hate
Is to say Scottie Pippen isn't an all-time great.

One real loser will try as hard as he can
To argue football with, of all people, Miami Dan.

But the greatest idiot, and he stands straight and tall,
Is the one who says Jamal Lewis can't run the ball.

And Rob, one last thing before I go—
Does what I've said describe someone we know?

What Next?

December 1, 2003

?

Attention Mid-Southerners, please be aware,
The dreaded Jeff Weinberger syndrome is in the air.

People who catch it often hear bells that don't ring
And then suddenly will say the dumbest thing.

It can be spread through the radio; I know this is true
Because of the Arkansas fan who called after LSU.

He said he saw positives, and then got his nose out of joint
When I said, "Great Scott, you got beat by 31 points."

It was, I thought, the absolute worst,
Until the next guy called and he was dumber than the first.

If you happen to catch it, please take note:
There is absolutely no known antidote.

So Heaven help you, because here's the scoop:
You'll be counting plastic points and watching ends loop.

Some Ideas Are Better Than Others
April 9, 2004

When I want to know what's up in the NBA,
All I do is open the mic and say,

"I need a call from L.A. Daniel." It's as simple as that,
And bingo—he pins Weinberger's shoulders to the mat.

He counts Kobe and Shaq among his circle of friends,
So his insight into the game never really ends.

Add his own native intellect, and it's plain to see,
He is the final authority, or so it seems to me.

Jeff doesn't agree, but the best he can do
Is to make some crack about Tyronn Lue.

So I'm gonna call Dr. Flinn and let him know
What we really need is the L.A. Daniel Show.

He'll cover the NBA and the big-time football schools,
And note when the SEC is caught breaking the rules.

What a great show—I'm already a fan,
And for a co-host, I'm gonna recommend Miami Dan.

Jack Eaton's Vocabulary 101
July 19, 2004

Here at the Sports Bar, I'm trying to find a way
For us all to learn a new word every day.

Apostasy is today's word, and you will see
There are those who think it applies to me.

It means to abandon a loyalty, throw it in the dumper,
Or in today's vernacular, a bandwagon jumper.

But I say unequivocally—here and now—
It is a charge that I vehemently disavow.

Next year, we Lakers fans will have our mettle tested,
But no need to worry, our loyalty is vested.

Friday's word will describe the SEC;
It's a three-syllable word—*dupery*.

Jack Eaton on Tiger Basketball

te TiGERS 1971-72

Where Are All the Tiger Fans

December 27, 1994

These days, anyone with even half a brain
Knows it's smart to avoid stress and strain.

But places like that are hard to find;
However, I do have a spot in mind.

If you want peace and quiet, as I recently did,
Go to a Tigers game at the Pyramid.

You can settle back without a care,
Because truthfully, there's no one there.

This lack of support is a constant worry,
And unless something is done in a real big hurry,

I can forsee exactly what lies in store,
A sign: Will the last fan out please lock the door?

The Way Things Are
January 10, 1995

It looks to me, from where I sit,
The best thing Deuce Ford did was quit.

It was obvious to me that in the main
He could run and shoot but mostly complain.

Larry was understanding all the while
And seemed to go the extra mile.

But somehow, the kid never learned
That playing time isn't given—it must be earned.

So—Go, Tigers. Go—play it fast and loose,
Because you've added tranquility by subtracting Deuce.

William Shakespeare and Jack Eaton
May 4, 1999

If Shakespeare were alive today he'd say, "Ah forsooth,
Tiger fans need to be lining up at the ticket booth."

Then he would add, "It's as sweet as honey
To see U of M fans spending their money."

I like the bard, and he knows whereof he speaks,
Because the season will be here in a matter of weeks.

And since the Tigers are coming off a dismal season,
That alone is the most important reason

To get behind the team and show your support,
So the guys can go out and hold the fort.

And as Bill would say, "You can get the job done
By dialing 678-2331."

Ode to the Commercial Appeal
December 22, 1999

I have often wondered, just what is the deal
When a newspaper is called the *Commercial Appeal*.

A commercial is an ad, at least it is to me,
While an appeal is just an obvious plea.

So the *Commercial Appeal*, to summarize,
Is one who begs people to advertise.

And when I read the paper, it's understood,
They sell those ads pretty good.

But today they took appeals to the next plateau;
They're begging for basketball fans, I want you to know.

Geoff Calkins wrote a column that had a critical tone,
Because at last night's Tigers game, he felt all alone.

The way I read it, no matter what else we did,
It was our duty to show up at the Pyramid.

Great Caesar's Ghost, this is something new–
The *CA* telling us what we should do.

Hey Geoff, with all due respect, please if you will–
Stick to reporting and being a shill.

The fans will be back, and you can put this in your file,
When the U of M gives them something worthwhile.

The U of M Coaching Situation
January 27, 2000

Johnny Jones or not Johnny Jones, is the question at hand,
And Tiger fans are getting in line to take a stand.

Some of them, after a detailed inspection,
Will contend we're going in the wrong direction.

While others will take a more defensive stance
And say, "Give the poor guy an honest chance."

For a while I thought the former was the way to go,
But I have been changing my mind ever so slow.

So instead of paying enough to ransom a king,
Let's give Johnny a chance to do his thing.

Someone's ox out there is bound to be gored,
But no one had heard of Gene Bartow 'til he came on board.

A John Calipari Poem

February 22, 2000

All the *T*s have been crossed and the *I*s have been dotted,
    And it seems that John Calipari has been slotted

To become the Tigers new head basketball man,
    At least that seems to be the latest plan.

Now, he's in no hurry to sign on and that's a pity,
    But first he says he wants to look over the city.

They're gonna pay him $900,000, plus a house and car.
    Is he a basketball coach or a top rock star?

As smart as he is, I'm sure he must know
    Interest in the program is at an all-time low.

And if he doesn't change things after a while,
    With all that money, at least he can leave in style.

Things Are Lookin' Good
March 13, 2000

Out at the U of M they have seen the light,
And finally, I think they have got it right.

The basketball program had hit a new low
So hiring John Calipari let everyone know

The Tigers are getting back in the game,
And Conference USA won't ever be the same.

First, I want to go to Cincinnati and make a case
That will wipe that smirk off Bob Huggins' face.

Then, so they know where we're coming from,
We'll do the same thing to Denny Crum.

And at the next conference tournament, get out of our way,
Because it ain't braggin' if you do what you say.

Ok coach, you get the players, put 'em to the test;
If you'll do that, the fans will take care of the rest.

Ode to Dajuan Wagner
March 23, 2000

Things will be looking up at the Pyramid
If the Tigers can just sign Milt Wagner's kid.

His name is Dajuan, and everybody knows
He will go where Arthur Barclay goes.

Arthur will be here this weekend to look around,
And if he likes the sights and the sound,

He just might say, "This suits me fine.
Where do I sign on the dotted line?"

Now, Dajuan's only a junior, so his signing day
Is still at least several months away.

But I, for one, am ready to state,
The kid is more than worth the wait.

Louisville wants Wagner really, really bad,
But I think the Cardinals have already been had.

And if Calipari pulls this off, it seems to me,
It'll be our biggest signing since we got Keith Lee.

It's Been a Tough Week
May 10, 2000

There is a comparison out there that I'd like to draw
That I hope will stick in every Louisville fan's craw.

It's the U of L versus the U of M,
And Milt Wagner saying, "It's us, not them."

However, the "us" isn't Louisville, no siree,
Because Milt is now a Tiger, you see.

Milt used to eat the Tigers for lunch,
But if you asked him now, I have a hunch

He would say with a huge amount of pride,
"Now I'm finally on the right side."

And there are guys who will pay a lot of dough
To hear Milt Wagner say, "Go Tigers. Go."

Ode to an Anti-fan

February 23, 2004

As I survey the situation from where I sit,
If there is such a thing as an anti-fan, I must be it.

I follow Louisville basketball, and this is true,
I don't hope they lose, but I'm glad when they do.

It's there in the record book, if anyone cares,
Their team beat my team more than my team beat theirs.

So when I read in the Sunday paper that they got beat,
Those sour grapes suddenly turned very sweet.

Then as I read on, I saw where they had taken a dive—
Of their last six games, they had been beaten in five.

This Saturday they'll play the Tigers in Freedom Hall,
And after contemplating the game, here's my call:

I expect the Tigers to play as hard as they can,
And win a big one for the Cardinal anti-fan.

On to the Final Four

April 5, 2008

Andre Allen won't play and that's a shame
But really he has only himself to blame.

Smoke a joint and you just might have to pay
Because random testing is the order of the day.

And with the zero tolerance policy like a doubled fist
Andre found himself on the suspended list.

But the outlook for the Tigers is not that bleak
And Coach Cal is surely not up the creek.

Because when Derrick Rose needs a blow
There is Willie Kemp ready to go.

I like our chances and won't it be fun
To beat the Bruins, after all we owe 'em one....

Ode to the Great Ones

April 7, 2008

When the Tigers line up tonight this much is known
They won't have to face the Jayhawks alone.

A lot of the old guys might have to struggle to hear it
They may not be there in person but surely in spirit.

Remember Mike Butler, there wasn't much he couldn't do
Add King George, Mackie Don and Deadeye Dexter too.

Look there's Keith Lee, Bobby Parks and also seen
Jimmy Hawkins, The Big Cat and hey–Clean Gene.

But the noblest of all sits alone in a trance
Please, Dear Lord is there even a chance

That as the seconds wind down and the spotlights glare
That somehow Larry Finch is made aware

That his boys have done it, they've gone all the way
And they stand as champions of all they survey.

So Go Tigers Go, the Red Sea has been parted
And Larry Finch is the one who got it all started.

A Second Chance

April 7, 2008

Bruins fans were cocky, they had paid their dues
And they could see no way that they could lose.

They had two superstars, each one double *O* tough
Surely, Kevin Love and Darren Collison would be more than enough.

But the Tigers also had some arrows in their quiver
After all CDR and Derrick Rose aren't exactly chopped liver.

The Tigers hit the ground running then poured on the coal
And by the second half they put it on cruise control.

Back in '73 in the final four we were soundly beaten
So here is the very latest according to Eaton;

I'm glad we whipped 'em but I want you to hear
I wish we could have stuck the ball in Bill Walton's ear....

A Loss to Gloat About

April 8, 2008

The loss to Kansas was tough but I always knew
That foul shooting would be our Waterloo.

We had a three point lead with seconds to play
And with an All-American at the line–he'd save the day.

He missed the first and our chances looked dim
As the second free throw bounced off the rim.

Kansas got the rebound and hurried up the floor
And a last second three pointer tied the score.

About the overtime the best that can be said
Is that the Tigers simply up and dropped dead.

But the ultimate indignity, and the bottom line cost
Are all those Tennessee fans who are glad we lost.

Ode To Coach Cal

April 27. 2008

When Coach Cal retires to be perfectly frank
He can either play lots of golf or open a bank.

His new contract calls for money galore
I think it equals the GDP of El Salvador.

But he earned it by accomplishing a tremendous feat
He has his Tigers up there with the nation's elite.

But now his problem as everyone well knows
Is to replace Joey, CDR and Derrick Rose.

But if past history can be used as a reliable guide
Coach Cal will scour the high schools far and wide.

And when recruiting is wrapped up there he'll be
Right up there with the nation's top two or three.

And back in Memphis Tiger fans will wonder why
The season can't start by the 4th of July...

Jack Eaton on Other Stuff

Ode to the World Cup
July 19, 1994

When it comes to the World Cup, please believe it–
    It is within my power to take it or leave it.

There were moments as exciting as I've ever seen,
    But they were just too far and few between.

The Americans did well, I was glad to see,
And I especially enjoyed the guy with the red goatee.

But now that it's over, all said and done;
Would you tell me please which team won?

Ode to the FESJC
August 2, 1994

As I watched the action ebb and flow,
I began rooting for a player I didn't know

His name was Dicky Pride, and as I watched from afar,
Was he a golfer or someplace to wash my car?

After three rounds, the other finally took heed,
Because at 13 under, he had a share of the lead.

As the final round started, he tightened his straps
And was determined to avoid a rookie collapse.

Dicky hung tough, it was a piece of cake,
As he made the shots he had to make.

Still—to win it all and reach his goal,
He had to play an extra hole.

So another FedEx is in the book,
And once again, I'll take a soulful look.

I'd have loved to have played, but I don't have the knack;
The desire is there, but it's the skills I lack.

So for the rest of my days I'll scheme and contrive,
But I'll never know the thrill of a John Daly drive.

Ode to Nascar
August 9, 1994

Over the years, I've tried as hard as I can
To become an honest-to-goodness NASCAR fan.

But there is one thing that doesn't seem fair–
They drive for hundreds of miles but don't go anywhere.

As I watch the race, without fail,
It reminds me of a dog chasing his tail.

And the terms are confusing, they're not very clear
For example, I once thought drafting was a keg of beer.

Ah, but there is one race I think would be fun–
It's from Memphis to Tunica on Route 61.

It Was a Travesty
May 2, 1995

Every once in a while I am compelled to report
On a horrible abuse in the world of sport.

For starters, I know there is always the chance
That wrestling winners are sometimes known in advance.

That's no big deal and part of the fun,
But to be perfectly honest, I'm a son of a gun.

I discovered that the old America's Cup
Makes wrestling look on the up and up.

The women won a race, but the men were no fools;
They simply went out and rewrote the rules.

So the ladies were robbed, and I hear their call,
It reminded me a whole lot of Freedom Hall.

To Put It Bluntly, The University of Indiana Sucks

May 16, 2000

No one at Indiana has the guts to face
That their University is now a total disgrace.

Coach Bobby Knight has survived another flap,
And the Board of Trustees put out the following crap.

One more miscue and that's all she wrote;
Someone will grab the coach by the throat.

And in the words of Shakespeare, the legendary bard,
"Knight will be hoisted by his own petard."

What that means, between you and me,
Knight will get just what he is due.

But I say, crapola, the next time someone's ox gets gored,
Knight will take over and he'll fire the board.

So every time the University swings, Knight just ducks,
And as I said, the University of Indiana just plain sucks.

A Poem About Nothing

February 6, 2001

Whenever a poet doesn't have a clue,
There is always one thing he or she can do.

Admit on the front end that there is no doubt–
You can't think of a single thing to write about.

Then go ahead and gripe and blow a gasket,
How we are all going to Hell in a new handbasket.

To complain about players' salaries is always cool,
And mention how today's kids don't learn anything in school.

And if there's still a blank after giving everything you've got,
You can't miss by giving Bill Clinton a shot.

Now all this won't win any prizes, but I will say,
You'll survive the drought and live to write another day.

Ode to My Favorite Golfer
July 9, 2001

As a bonafide, certified Tiger Woods freak,
I expect him to win every single week.

A tournament used to be a sure slam dunk,
But lately Tiger's been in a real blue funk.

Things have been so bad that I'm sure you know,
He's been out of the top ten three times in a row.

And yesterday he was way, way off the pace;
He was 13 shots back, in 20th place.

The British Open is next in Tiger's sight,
And if things pick up and go just right,

He'll hop right out of his current rut;
He'll hit every green and hole every putt.

And the natural order of things will be restored
As Tiger resumes his place atop the leaderboard.

Goodbye to Money

May 26. 2008

The price of gas is out of sight
And from what I hear it even might;

Go even higher and if that's the case
The motoring public may have to face,

That since the oil companies feel no remorse
We all may have to get a horse.

So, we get a horse and everything we need
And then just watch the price of feed.

So, what I'm about to say may sound funny
But I think it's a conspiracy to get our money.

Now, I certainly don't want to be thought of as rude
But I think the American people are getting screwed.

Memphis TV News
July 29, 2008

Check any Memphis station at ten and I'll make you a bet
That this is just about what you'll get.

A shooting in South Memphis and then for good measure
Another one plus a car jacking somewhere in Frayser.

A home invasion in Germantown and likely as not
A guy from Collierville is robbed in the Kroger parking lot.

There are meth labs galore and right in between
Gang graffiti where it simply should not be seen.

The cops are working hard but only a dunce
Could think they could be in two places at once.

I'm as sick of it as you are and it's such a pity
But that's what's happening right here in River City.

Now, I know this won't cut the rate of crime
But I wish TV5 would give Jarvis a little more time...

Olympic Basketball - U.S. vs. China
August 14, 2008

The Chinese language so it's been said
Has no translation for "upside the head."

And that's too bad because like it or not
That's just exactly what they got.

The Communists started fast if you please
And stayed close to the Americans by hitting three's.

But in the second half the U.S. had it made
As Bryant played well–so did James and Wade.

Some Chinese fans got their nose out of joint
As their team was smoked by 31 points.

31 points–Great Scott–the Commies were dead
And in any language they got hit–upside the head.

What to do with the Pyramid

August 14, 2008

I am now ready to submit my bid
As to what we should do with the Pyramid.

First of all we can no longer wait
So let's tell Bass Pro to fish or cut bait.

Better yet you wanna know what
Tell them don't let the door bust your butt.

Then tell all the politicians to take a hike
And let some businessmen tell us what they would like.

They would say we would all do very well
With a Tunica style casino and a luxury hotel.

This would put our system under the gun
Because it's a whole lot easier said than done.

We'd need the state legislature to get on board
And here's where we would miss good 'ol John Ford.

That's my idea and I'm telling you
Other people will have to see it through.

Olympic Wrap-Up
August 24, 2008

At this point in time there is little doubt
That I have had it, I am Olympiced out.

I was with Michael Phelps every inch of the way
While he was tired I was exhausted at the end of the day.

Our basketball team was a welcome reprieve
At the half we'd won and I could usually leave.

Soccer was a bummer but I always understood
On the Olympic stage we rarely did any good.

I can't get with diving and I'm not sure why
But in 2012 I'll give it another try.

Boat races are boring but I gotta think
It would jazz it up if one would sink.

Water polo and ping pong bore me to tears
I have avoided them like the plague over the years.

But to me the verdict was signed and sealed
I do like track but I can't stand field.

So the Olympics are over and I'll say this
It is one thing on TV that I will not miss.

Jack Eaton with the Last Word for Tiger Fans

A Tiger Fan's Benediction
August 14, 2008

Life's journey is short and the end is near
But I face eternity with a conscience that's clear.

I have loved the Almighty and studied his word
And what I say next I hope will be heard:

The road to Heaven is laid out, it's easily seen
Book of John–Chapter 3, Verse 16.

So I say, "REPENT." Do it now or surely you will
Spend eternity in Freedom Hall in Louisville.

glossary

A-Rod (see Rodriguez, Alex)

Abdul "What's-His-Name" (see Abdur-Rahim, Shareef)

Abdur-Raheem, Shareef - A good trade.

Ainge, Erik - UT quarterback.

Air McNair (see McNair, Steve)

Albert (see Means, Albert)

Allen, Andre - You don't make a point by smoking a joint.

Archie (see Manning, Archie)

Bill (for "William Shakespeare and Jack Eaton" see Shakespeare, William or for "Ode To Bill and Hillary" see Clinton, Bill)

Barclay, Arthur - The kid we signed to get Dajuan Wagner.

Bartow, Gene - Coach of Tigers basketball in the early seventies.

Battier, Shane - The city's favorite Grizzlies player to date.

Bibby, Mike - Inherited from Vancouver and traded just as fast.

Big Country (see Reeves, Bryant)

Brown, Hubie - Knows more basketball than anyone who ever lived or who ever will live. He is a walking encyclopedia–a master of the game. I once asked him a question and didn't understand his answer, although I said I did. I didn't want him to think I was dumb..

Bryant, Kobe- Wish we had him.

Butler, Mike - One of my favorites. A hot dog's hot dog. Great shooter–great everything. Played for Moe Iba–nuff said.

Calipari, John - Will take the Tigers where no one has taken them before. He is "in a class by hisself" as Coach Murphy would say.

Calkins, Geoff - Best CA writer since Lydel Sims.

CDR (see Chris Douglas-Roberts)

Chris Douglas-Roberts - Money.

Clausen, Casey - UT quarterback and Peyton Manning wannabe. He was OK.

Clean Gene (see Gene Bartow)

Clinton, Bill - Former President and political sleeze.

Coach Cal (see Calipari, John)

Coker, Larry - Miami Dan never did like this guy. Won with other coach's players.

Collison, Darren - Not really as much help for UCLA as the "experts" assumed.

Cox, Bobby - Braves manager. Must be good–Weinberger doesn't like him.

Crum, Denny - Louisville head coach for a hundred years or so.

Daly, John - Really hits the cover off the ball.

Dan (see Miami Dan)

Deadeye Dexter (see Reed, Dexter)

Dennis (see Rodman, Dennis)

DiMaggio, Joe - Did a great coffee commercial. Also played some center field. Hall of famer.

Dorsey, Joey - A man among boys.

Dr. Flinn - The owner of Sports56.

Dr. Spock - A great baby man. Never appeared on Star Trek.

Dunn, Joe Lee - How has the Tigers "D" done since Joe Lee was canned.

Eaton, Jack - The author of the greatest book of poems you are reading right now.

Eddie (see George, Eddie)

Elli (see Manning, Eli)

Fisher, Rob - Radio talk show host at Sports56.

Finch, Larry - It ain't even close. All time #1 for the Tigers.

Ford, Deuce - Not a car... Quit the U of M basketball team.

Ford Sr., Harold - U.S. Representative from Tennessee and brother to John Ford.

Ford, John - Tennessee State Senator accused of taking bribes to get legislation passed.

Ford, Ophelia - Younger sister of John Ford and anemic Tennessee Senator.

Fulmer, Phil - UT Football coach.

Gasol, Pau - Best player the Grizzlies have had (so far).

George, Eddie - Oilers/Titans running back and Heisman trophy winner.

Greer, Jarvis - I taught him everything I know.

Harold Sr. (see Ford, Harold Sr.)

Hardaway, Anfernee - The most successful NBA player ever to come out of Memphis.

Hawkins, Jimmy - A stud from Treadwell who played with Mike Butler–of Kingsbury at Memphis State.

Henry, Travis - Shared the UT backfield with Jamal Lewis.

Herenton, Willie - Mayor of Memphis for what seems like a thousand years.

Hillary - The wife of former President Bill Clinton.

Houston, Cedric - A three-year starting running back at UT.

Hubie (see Brown, Hubie)

Huggins, Bob - A coach Tiger fans love to hate..and for good reason.

Hussein, Saddam - Leader of Iraq, until U.S took over.

J. Will (see Williams, Jason)Jack (see Eaton, Jack)

Jack (see Eaton, Jack)

Jackson, Jesse - Civil rights activist.

Jackson, Phil - Coach of the Michael Jordan Championships as well as the Kobe
Bryant Championships.

James, Edgerrin - The monster running back for the Indianapolis Colts.

James, Lebron - Cleveland Cavaliers star won Olympic gold.

Jarvis (see Greer, Jarvis)

Jeff (see Weinberger, Jeff)

Jeff and Jack Radio Show - I am amazed at how many people remember the show. People quote things for me all the time. The most popular quote, "Weinberger is an idiot." We are available at a moments notice for another radio gig.

Jerry (see West, Jerry)

Joe (see DiMaggio, Joe)

Joe Lee (see Dunn, Joe Lee)

Joey (see Dorsey, Joey)

John (see John Ford)

Jones, Johnny - Never given a real opportunity to coach Memphis basketball.

Jordan, Michael - Basketball genius.

Kobe (see Bryant, Kobe)

Knight, Bobby - Player choker.

Kemp, Willie - A solid backup that can hit a three occasionally.

King George (see Kirk, George)

King "What's-His-Name" - King Solomon.

Kirk, George - the first kid I ever gave a nick name to–King George the First of Memphis State. Tough, hard-nosed and played point guard before there were point guards.

L.A. Daniel - Probably the smartest caller to our radio show. Would call Jeff Weinberger an idiot and then prove it. Brilliant mind.

Lasorda, Tommy - Player, coach, manager in some capacity for the Dodgers since 1954.

Lee, Keith - The Tigers would not have made a ripple in the 80's with out Keith. I love this kid. He was magnificent or better.

Lewis, Jamal - #31 at UT. #31 at Baltimore and #31 at Cleveland. I wish we (the Steelers) had him.

Lexington Steve - West Tennessee's biggest UT fan. Once called Tiger basketball–crap.

Lue Tyronn - Lakers guard who won two championships in his first three seasons.

Logan (see Young, Logan)

Love, Kevin - The supposed savior for UCLA.

Lowe, Sidney - The first coach of the "Memphis" Grizzlies.

King Willie (see Herenton, Willie)

Mackie Don (see Smith, Mackie Don)

Madkin, Wayne - The winningest QB in the SEC in the early 2000's. He was Double O tough. The best QB at Mississippi State since Rocky Felker.

Manning, Archie - Head of the Manning clan. A great quarterback in his own right but he pales in comparison to his kids, Peyton and Eli.

Manning, Eli - Archie's other kid won the Super Bowl. Hallaeujah!

McGuire, Mark - Nicest home run champion in decades.

Manning, Peyton - The QB for the Indianapolis Colts and former QB for the UT Vols.

Martin, Tee - Did for UT what Peyton Manning could not do. Win the big one. NCAA champs.

Maz (see Mazeroski, Bill)

Mazeroski, Bill - Pirate hall of famer. Hit walk off home run to beat the Yankees in 1960 World Series. Best second baseman ever–in Pittsburgh.

McNair, Steve - Quarterback who helped bring Tennessee to the Super Bowl.

Means, Albert - Brought talk of a salary cap for the SEC. $200,000 for a defensive tackle–things are getting out of hand.

Miami Dan - Weinberger's nemesis. Dan thinks the SEC cheats. He'd prove his point every time he called the radio show. Brilliant football mind.

Michael (see Jordan, Michael)

Miller, Romero - Record-setting quarterback at Ole Mis before Eli Manning came along.

Moses - Led the ancient tribes from Egypt to the Promised Land.

Murphy, Billy "Spook" - Winningest football coach at Memphis State. Tough minded ex-Marine, but inside was a pussy cat. I knew him for many years and can't think of a negative thing to say about him—Oh, yes—His tires were always under inflated.

Napoleon - The French ruler who met his end in Belgium in 1815.

Neyland, General Robert R. - Former coach at UT for whom Neyland Stadium was named after.

O'Neal, Shaquille - NBA center for the Orlando Magic before moving to the L.A. Lakers

Ostertag, Greg - Jeff's idea of a great center

Parker, Tony - A Frenchman and a basketball player.

Parks, Bobby - Shooting guard under Dana Kirk in the early eighties.

Patton, General George S. - A real american hero. At Kasserine Pass, he whipped General Rommel and said, "I read your book." George C. Scott won an Oscar playing him in the movies. The best flick I ever saw.

Pau (see Gasol, Pau)

Payton, Gary - Also known as "The Glove"

Penny (see Hardaway, Anfernee)

Phelps, Michael - Aquaman.

Pippen, Scottie - An all-time great.

Pride, Dicky - Won the 1994 FedEx St. Jude Classic.

Ragsdale, Duncan - Memphis-area attorney.

Reed, Dexter - Left handed whiz. Had one assist in his career—the ball slipped out of his hand as he was taking a shot. I'm kidding, Deadeye!!!!

Reeves, Bryant - The honorable thing to do-give the Grizzlies their money back. Who ever drafted this guy, anyway.

Rob (see Fisher, Rob)

Robinson, Ronnie - The Big Cat. Once grabbed 28 rebounds in a single game. He and Larry Finch were Tiger basketball. May he rest in peace.

Rodman, Dennis - A flamboyant, rebounder. I emphasize flamboyant.

Rodriguez, Alex - Makes more than the whole Pirates team-but he didn't make the playoffs either!

Rose, Derrick - I don't need to explain this one.

Saddam (see Hussein, Saddam)

Shakespeare, William - Wrote a lot of rhymes–like me.

Shane (see Battier, Shane)

Shaq (see O'Neal, Shaquille)

Spurrier, Steve - Head coach at Florida for more than ten years.

Sonny Boy Shelby - What a great guy–student, teacher, coach, musician, and war hero. I once asked him who he was pulling for in an upcoming football game. He said, "I gotta be for Ole Miss, after all they done gimme my education." You gotta love a guy like that. May he rest in peace.

Smith, Dean - North Carolina legendary coach.

Smith, Fred - Richest man in Memphis and the owner of FedEx.

Smith, Mackie Don - Or just simply "Mackie Don." Six foot eight and could shoot lights out. Good kid!

Sprewell, Latrell - Suspended for 82 games for choking his coach, P.J. Carlesimo.

Strawberry, Darryl - One of the most feared sluggers in the game.

Stromile (see Swift, Stromile)

Swift, Stromile - Grizzlies power forward who Weinberger wanted to trade away.

Tagliabuc, Paul - NFL Commissioner from 1989 to 2006.

Ted (see Williams, Ted)

Tell, William - An archer who shot at apples.

The Big Cat (see Robinson, Ronnie)

Tommy (see Lasorda, Tommy)

Wade, Dwyane - Miami Heat star won Olympic Gold.

Wagner, Milt - Cardinal turned Tiger assistant coach and father of Dajuan Wagner.

Walton, Bill - I know he dunked the ball a few times in '73.

Wayne (see Madkin, Wayne)

Webber, Chris - A member of the Fab Five.

Weinberger, Jeff - He thinks he is the final authority on just about everything. Truth is–as Coach Murphy would say–He don't know squat. He is a great talk show host because he makes the listeners so angry.

West, Jerry - The logo.

Williams, Jason - An exciting point guard who once stole a pen from Geoff Calkins.

Williams, Ted - I interviewed him once. He was gracious and answered my dumb questions like a pro.

Willie (see Herenton, Willie)

Willie the Chicken (see Herenton, Willie)

Willlingham, John - If he had been elected mayor, this city would not be in the shape it's in. A smart guy who would make all the difference in the world.

Wimprine, Danny - Memphis quarterback from 2001-2004.

Woods, Tiger - the greatest golfer to have ever lived.

Wright, Lorenzen - Tiger basketball center who later became a Grizzlies center.

Young, Logan - Memphis rich guy who was Alabama's money guy. He went to Vanderbilt but I guess even he couldn't save the Commodores.

Zook, Ron - Coach who took over at Florida after Steve Spurrier resigned.

Zow, Andrew - Crimson Tide quarterback from 1998-2000.